[*PLEASE READ AND CIRCULATE.*]

AN

INSIDE VIEW

OF

HE REBELLION,

AND

AMERICAN CITIZEN'S TEXT-BOOK.

BY

HENRY CONKLING, M. D.,

BLOOMINGTON, ILL.

INSIDE VIEW OF THE REBELLION.

Ques.—What are the views and feelings of the people of the North in regard to the rebellion?

Ans.—They are divided into two classes: First, those who are in favor of prosecuting the war and sustaining the Administration. Second, those who are against the Administration and the war, and in favor of making peace with the rebels.

Ques.—Who are included in the first class?

Ans.—Republicans and Democrats, or, as they are called, War Democrats.

Ques.—Who are included in the second class?

Ans.—Conservatives, Anti-War Democrats, Rebel Sympathizers and Traitors.

Ques.—Are not the Conservatives a separate and distinct party, who are working for the good of the Union and the subjugation of the rebels?

Ans.—Not at all; their doctrines and teachings harmonize with the Anti-War Democrats and Rebel Sympathizers.

Ques.—What are the teachings of these parties, and how are they understood?

Ans.—Their records are clear, as will be shown for your consideration:

Record of Republicans and War Democrats.

Resolution of the Union mass Convention of Illinois, held at Springfield, Sept. 3rd, 1863.

"*Resolved, That we are in favor of the further offensive prosecution of the war,* because we believe it is the only way to crush out this rebellion, and because we do not believe that its further offensive prosecution tends to anarchy or misrule, but the speedy overthrow of the rebellion and the permanent re-establishment of the government and on an honorable basis."

At an immense Union meeting composed of Republicans and War Democrats, held in Philadelphia, March 11th, 1863, the following resolutions were adopted:

"*Resolved,* That no calamity could befall the American people so terrible in its results, as the breaking up of the foundation of the Government of the United States, and under a solemn sense of duty to God and our country, we therefore pledge to each other, our sacred honor *to sustain the President and its other constituted authorities* in their efforts to overwhelm and subjugate its enemies by force of arms, and all the appliances of war, as the only means of restoring its sovereign authority under the Constitution, securing the blessings of peace, and preserving the liberties of the people."

"*Resolved,* That in this momentous struggle in which the nation is now engaged, we have a common and undivided interest, *with our patriotic armies in the field* and all who value the proud title of American citizens in maintaining the honor of its flag and the unity of its Government, and we greet all

Record of Conservatives, Anti-War Democrats, Rebel sympathizers, and Traitors.

Resolution of the Anti-War State Convention, held at Springfield Illinois, June 17th, 1863.

"*Resolved, That we are opposed* to the further offensive prosecution of the war, as tending to subvert the Constitution and the Government, and entail upon this nation all the disastrous consequences of misrule and anarchy."

At an Anti-War Tory Democratic meeting, held in Edgar county, Illinois, 4th of July, 1863, the following resolution was adopted:

"*Resolved,* That we hereby undividedly pledge ourselves one to another, that *we will not render support to the present Administration* in carrying on the abolition crusade against the South.

"That we will resist to the death, all attempts *to draft any of our citizens into the army,* and that we will permit no arbitrary arrests to be made among us by the minions of the Administration."

W. W. Eaton, one of the leading spirits of a democratic convention which nominated *Seymour for " Governor,"* in a closing speech said, "The doings of this convention *will awake lively emotions in the South.* The resolutions we have adopted will cause a thrill in the hearts of the *Southern Brethren.*

such citizens of every tongue, kindred and persuasion throughout the land, as our friends and brethren in a righteous cause, and we earnestly invoke their stern rebuke of *every treasonable suggestion* to abandon the contest and their active aid in proclaiming to foreign powers and domestic foes, the irrevocable will of the American people *that the Union must and shall be preserved.*

At a Union meeting, held in the "Cooper Institute," New York, Oct., 1862, at which meeting several exiles from the South were present and addressed the meeting, the following resolutions were adopted:

"Whereas, The present Chief Magistrate is using all constitutional means to put down this rebellion, restore peace to the country, and bring the leaders of this unparalleled treason against free institutions to condign punishment, therefore

"*Resolved,* That any terms of compromise or of peace, short of an unconditional surrender of the rebels to the authority of the United States would be degrading to the sovereignty, and destructive of the rights and liberties of all loyal citizens of the South."

"*Resolved, That the salvation of the Union depends on a vigorous prosecution of the War,* until the stars and stripes wave triumphantly from the Canadas to the Gulf, and from ocean to ocean."

Senator Douglas, (War Democrat,) said in his last legacy to the Democratic party, May 10, 1861:

"All hope of compromise with the cotton States was abandoned, when they assumed the position that the separation of the Union was complete and final, and that they never would consent to a reconstruction in any contingency, *not even if we would furnish them with a blank sheet of paper, and permit them to inscribe their own terms.*

"In view of this state of things, there was but one path of duty left to patriotic men. *It was not a party question, nor a question involving partizan policy; it was a question of Government or No Government, Country or no Country; and hence it became the imperative duty of every Union man,* every friend of constitutional liberty, to rally to the support of our common country, its Government and flag; as the only means of checking the progress of the revolution, and preserving the Union of the States. *I trust the time will never come when I shall not be willing to make any sacrifice of personal feeling and party feeling and party policy, for the honor and integrity of my country.*"

The "Louisville Democrat," (War) a leading Democratic paper of Kentucky, says

"There can be no true democracy, while treason keeps its armies in the field, except *T. H. Seymour* is a man whom the brave men and lovely women of the South love, honor and esteem. *The conservative men of the North will grasp the demon Abolition by the throat, strangle it, and invite our brethren of the South to unite with us.*

The "New York News" (Tory) submits the following plan in a recent issue:

"*In leagueing with the War Democracy, they do not volunteer for a prosecution of the war; their mission in the campaign is to defeat Black Republicanism,* and on *that point they accord* with the War Democracy. When Black Republicanism shall have vanished *before the united strength of the Peace and War Democrats, then will come the hour to confront the War Democracy and give them battle upon the direct* issue. It is the duty of the peace party to exert themselves as strenuously as if one sentiment animated themselves and their co-adjutors. A victory over Black Republicanism is the first step towards a triumph of the peace sentiment. We *must attempt that step, however distasteful may be the companionship of those who lack our sympathy on the war question.* We do not yield our advocacy of peace, but simply hold that issue in reserve."

Extract of Lord Lyons' letter to Earl Russell:

WASHINGTON, Nov. 17, 1862.

MY LORD: On my arrival at New York, on the 8th instant, *I found the conservative leaders exulting in the crowning success achieved by the party in that State.*

On the following morning, however, intelligence arrived from Washington, *which dashed the rising hopes of the conservatives.*

It was announced that General McClellan had been dismissed from command of the army of the Potomac, and ordered to repair to his home.

The General had been regarded as the representative of the conservative principle in the army. Support of him had been made one of the articles of the conservative electoral programme.

Several of the leaders of the Democratic party sought interviews with me both before and after the arrival of the intelligence of General McClellan's dismissal.

The subject uppermost in their minds while they were speaking to me, was naturally that of foreign mediation between North and South.

Many of them seemed to think that the mediation must come at last, *but they appeared to be very much afraid of its coming too soon.*

They appeared to regard the present moment as peculiarly unfavorable for such an offer, and indeed, to hold, *that it would be*

'War Democracy.' The office hunters who at a time like this, *preach peace, peace*, in the North may be democrats in name, ☞ but in reality they are traitors and Tories who would be in arms against their Government were they living in the so-called Confederacy." ☜

essential to the success of any proposal from abroad that it should be deferred until the control of the Executive Government should be in the hands of the Conservative party.

Pledge of the Loyal National League.

"We, the undersigned citizens of the United States, hereby associate ourselves under the name and title of the Loyal National League.

☞ "We pledge ourselves to an unconditional loyalty to the Government of the United States ☜ to an unwavering support of its efforts to suppress the rebellion, and to spare no endeavor to maintain unimpaired the National Unity, both in principle and in territorial boundary. The primary object of this league is and shall be to bind together all loyal men of all trades and professions in a common union to maintain the power, glory and integrity of the Union."

The following is part of the oath of the "Knights of the Golden Circle:"

The candidate having his hand on the Bible, is asked:

"Do you believe this to be the word of God, and do you believe the present war now being waged against us to be unconstitutional."

Both being answered in the affirmative, the candidate takes the following oath:

"I promise and swear that I will do all in my power to bring all loyal Democrats into this circle of hosts; and I further promise and swear, ☞ that I will do all in my power against the present Yankee disunion Administration; so help me God." ☜

Ques.—Do not the Anti-War, Conservative Democrats charge this war upon the Abolitionists?

Ans.—They do. In May, 1862, some of the Democratic members of Congress issued an address to the people of the United States, in which may be found the following language: "The bitter waters of secession flowed first and are fed still from the unclean fountain of Abolitionism. Armies may break down the power of the Confederate Government of the South, but the work of restoration can only be carried on through political organizations. In this great work, we cordially invite the co-operation of all men of every party, who are opposed to the fell spirit of Abolitionism."

Ques.—Can you give the definition of an Abolitionist?

Ans.—We can; from two authorities which the Anti-War Conservatives cannot object to:

Definition of an Abolitionist from Chicago Times (Tory.)

"He who supports the war is against the Union, because the war is the most terrible engine for the destruction of the Union which Belzebub himself could have invented; *the professed Democrat, therefore, who has his senses about him, and is deliberately for the war, is* NOT *a Democrat in fact, but an Abolitionist of the most radical, violent and destructive kind.*"

Definition of an Abolitionist, from the Richmond Literary Messenger (Secesh.)

"An Abolitionist is any man who does not love slavery for its own sake as a divine institution, who does not worship it as the corner stone of civil liberty, who does not adore it as the only possible social condition on which a permanent Republican Government can be created, and who does not in his inmost soul desire to see it extended and perpetuated over the whole earth, as a means of human reformation, second in dignity and importance to the Christian religion. Who does not love African slavery with this love is an Abolitionist."

Ques.—Reader, are you for prosecuting the war and subduing the rebels? if you say Yes, then you are an Abolitionist of the most radical kind, so says the *Chicago Times*, and it is the text-book for the Anti-War, Conservative Tory Democrats.

Ques.—Do you believe that slavery is a Divine institution, and can you adore it as the corner stone of civil liberty, and second in dignity and importance to the Christian religion? If you do not thus love slavery, *then you are an Abolitionist*—so says the *Literary Messenger*.

Ques.—Which one of these horns will you lay hold upon?

Ans.—I will lay hold upon neither; but will contend for the Flag of the Union, and Freedom.

Having shown that the people of the North are divided into two classes, and the doctrines taught by them, we will now pass on to show

1st. That the rebellion was inaugurated under James Buchanan's administration, although it had been in contemplation some time previous.

2d. That the people of the South had not been deprived of any of their rights which caused them to rebel.

3d. Show what were the real designs of the South in rebelling and establishing a separate Government.

4th. The rebellion as presented under Mr. Lincoln's administration, and the difficulties surrounding him.

5th. The policy adopted under his administration for suppressing the rebellion.

6th. The reason the rebellion has not long since been subdued; and

7th. Prove by their own record that the rebels spurn with contempt any propositions of compromise coming from the North, *save that of a recognition of their independence.*

Ques.—How long before the expiration of James Buchanan's term as President of the United States had the rebellion been in progress?

Ans.—About three months.

Ques.—What progress had the South made in that time?

Ans.—The State of South Carolina, Georgia, Alabama, Mississippi, Louisiana and Florida had seceded, and all their forts, arsenals, dock yards and custom houses had been seized and held in open hostility to the Government, except Fort Pickens, Taylor, Jefferson and Sumter.

Ques.—Did James Buchanan, as President of the United States, use the means within his power to suppress the rebellion?

Ans.—He did not; for his views and feelings were with the South.

Ques.—Have we any evidence of this?

Ans.—The 16th of March, 1850, he wrote a letter to Jefferson Davis, in which he used the following language: "I first went to Congress in December, 1821, and throughout my whole public career have been uniform in maintaining the just Constitutional rights of the South. I shall be assailed as long as I live *for having gone further in support of the South than Southern Senators and Representatives.* I am committed to the Missouri Compromise, and that Compromise shall stand; under these circumstances, it would be madness in me to take higher ground for the South than they have taken for themselves, this would be to out-Herod Herod, and to be more Southern than the South."

Ques.—What other evidence have we?

Ans.—The special Message of James Buchanan that was sent to Congress on 9th January, 1861. The most important feature of the document is in regard to the rebellion, in which he says: "*The right and duty to use the military and naval forces against those who illegally assail the Government, are clear and indisputable.*" But he considers the present state of things revolutionary, and *beyond Executive control*, and throws the whole responsibility of action upon Congress. He alleges as a reason for not sending reinforcements to Major Anderson, "that such an action would have furnished a pretext, if not the provocation, for aggression on the part of South Carolina."

Ques.—How long before this Message was sent to Congress had South Carolina passed a secession ordinance?

Ans.—About three weeks.

Ques.—Who was Secretary of War under Buchanan?

Ans.—John B. Floyd.

Ques.—How many fire arms did he send South under one order?

Ans.—One hundred and fifteen thousand.

Ques.—What evidence have we of this?

Ans.—The *Richmond Examiner*, at one time the mouth-piece of Floyd, says: "The facts we are about to state *are official and indisputable.* Under a single order of the late Secretary of War, John B. Floyd, made during the last year, there was one hundred and fifteen thousand improved muskets and rifles transferred from the Springfield Armory and Watervelet Arsenal to different arsenals at the South; what numbers were supplied by other and minor orders, and what numbers of improved arms had before the great order been deposited in the South, cannot now be ascertained."

Ques.—What other evidences is there?

Ans.—The testimony of Gen. Scott, who said in an official report, made to President Lincoln, March 30, 1861, "that in view of the meditated rebellion, Floyd had ordered one hundred and fifteen thousand muskets and rifles from Northern depositories to Southern arsenals."

Ques.—How was John B. Floyd rewarded for his treachery?

Ans.—By being appointed Brigadier General in the rebel army.

Ques.—Had the South premeditated a rebellion and a separate Government?

Ans.—The doctrine of secession was advocated as early as 1790. A letter was written April 5, 1790, by Robert B. Lee, grandfather of the present commander-in-chief of the rebel army, in which the writer makes use of the following language: "The Southern States are too weak at present to stand by themselves, but when we shall attain our natural degree of population, I flatter myself that we ☞ shall have the power to do ourselves justice with dissolving the bond that binds us together."

The *Richmond Examiner* says in regard to the rebellion: "It has taken forty years to bring it about."

Andrew Jackson wrote a letter to Andrew J. Crawford, May 1, 1833, in these words; "The tariff was only the pretext with the South, while disunion and a Southern Confederacy the real object. The next pretext will be the *negro or slavery question.*"

Ques.—Have we any other evidence?

Ans.—J. M. Mason, United States Senator from Virginia, wrote a letter to Jefferson Davis, September 30, 1856, in which he says: "I have a letter from Wise, of the 27th, full of spirit. He says the Governors of North Carolina, South Carolina and Louisiana have already agreed to meet at Raleigh, and others will. *This you will keep secret.* He says further, that he had officially requested you to exchange with Virginia, on fair terms of difference, percussion for flint muskets. Virginia, probably, has more arms than the other Southern States, and would divide in case of need. In a letter yesterday to a committee in South Carolina, ☞ I gave it as my judgment in case of Fremont's election, the South should not pause, but proceed at once to immediate, absolute and eternal separation. So I am a candidate for the first halter. ☜ Wise says, accounts from Philadelphia are cheering for *Old Buchanan* in Pennsylvania. I hope they be not delusive."

Ques.—What position did *Wise* hold at this time?

Ans.—He was Governor of Virginia.

Ques.—What position did Jefferson Davis hold when this letter was sent to him by Mason?

Ans.—He was Secretary of War under Franklin Pierce.

Ques.—Were Buchanan and Fremont candidates for President at this time?

Ans.—They were.

Take notice, reader, that Mason, Davis and Wise were plotting with the Governors of North Carolina, South Carolina and Louisiana, to overthrow the Government in 1856, *in case Fremont was elected.*

Ques.—Had the people of the South been deprived of any of their rights, which caused them to rebel and establish a separate Government?

Ans.—They had no just cause of complaint.

Ques.—What evidence of this have we?

Ans.—There is abundant testimony, to which we call your attention.

Thomas H. Hicks, Governor of Maryland, and a slaveholder, published an address in January, 1861, to the citizens of that State, in which he used the following language: "I firmly believe that a division of the Government will inevitably produce a civil war. We are told by the leading spirits of the South Carolina Convention, ☞ that neither the election of Mr. Lincoln, nor the non-execution of the fugitive slave law, nor both combined, constitute their grievances. They declare that the real cause of their discontent dates back as far as 1833." ☜

Ex-Governor Stewart introduced in 1861, a resolution in the Missouri Convention, saying: "That no overt act had been committed by the Federal Government to justify either nullification, secession or revolution."

Andrew Johnson, of Tennessee, delivered an address to the Third Minnesota Regiment, near Nashville, in February, 1862, in which he said: "He knew the leaders of this rebellion well, both personally and politically, and he declared it was the firm determination of the rebel leaders to overthrow popular Government, and establish a despotism instead of our present liberal institutions, ☞ and that the people of the South would not submit to a President who had sprung from the *common people as Abe Lincoln had.*"

Parson Brownlow, of Tennessee, said in a speech in 1862: "*The South had no cause to complain.* With half the States and Territories and half the population of the North, they have had thirteen out of nineteen Presidents, five of whom occupied the Presidential chair forty years.

When the Crittenden propositions were before Congress in December, 1860, Senator Iverson, of Georgia, held the following language: "Sir, the Southern States that are moving in this matter, are not doing it without due consideration. ☞ We don't suppose there will be any overt acts on the part of Mr. Lincoln. We do not propose to wait for them; we intend to go out."

Pryor, of Virginia, telegraphed from Washington to Richmond: "**We can get the** Crittenden Compromise, *but we don't want it.*"

Stephen A. Douglas said in his Springfield speech, April 27, 1861: "For the first time since the adoption of the Federal Constitution a wide-spread conspiracy exists to destroy the best Government the sun of Heaven ever shed its rays upon. The simple question presented to us is, whether we shall wait for the enemy to carry out his boasts of making war upon our soil. ☞ I ask you to reflect, and then point out any one act that has been done and any one duty that has been omitted to be done, of which any one of these disunionists can justly complain."

Having shown that the South had no just cause of complaint, the question arises what *were* the real designs of the South in establishing a separate Government?

Ans.—Two objects were contemplated in establishing a Southern Confederacy—

1st. An Oligarchy or Monarchy; and

2d. The perpetuation of slavery.

Ques.—Have we positive evidence of this?

Ans.—We have; as their own speeches and writings will testify. A letter was sent to the French Court, November, 1862, signed by Jefferson Davis and seventy-three of the leading men of the South, urging of the Emperor a speedy recognition of the South, and offering the following inducements to Napoleon: 1st. That it is the intention of the leaders of the South, (which intention is to be kept secret until the war is over,) as soon as their independence was declared, to establish a *Nobility* in the South before the army was disbanded. That the poor whites or non slave owners, who would help them fight and conquer their independence, so soon as a Nobility is established, and they are left free to act, will emigrate North and leave *only the Noble and his slave.* Constituting the firmest Nobility, *because the Peasant will be the property of the Noble*, while the line of demarcation between them will be that of color and race; that their ability so to establish a Nobility cannot be doubtful, when it is well known that the leaders of the South had enforced this war and established the present Confederacy.

Ques.—Has not the above declaration been published for party effect without any just foundation?

Ans.—Not at all. We will offer other good evidence to substantiate the above. The following extract is taken from the Southern "Literary Messenger," published in Richmond, Virginia. "*That benign institution of Slavery which is now the pride and glory of the South*, to ascribe to the conception of Divinity the great element of power in the Confederacy, will prove in preventing too heavy an influx from foreign shores of that class of population devoted to menial pursuits; let us seek at once to eradicate every vestage of Radical Democracy, every feature tending to make us a popular Government; let us learn from history that popular principles are but poor guarantees to liberty. *We have no special objection to royalty* when restrained by constitutional barriers; ☞ certainly the condition of a subject of the Czar of Russia, the most absolute monarchies, is preferable to that of a democratic government. ☜ No foreigner who comes amongst us after the struggle is over should ever enjoy the elective franchise."

In the "Richmond Whig," of June, 1862, is found the following language: "The experience of the war is an attestation of the truth long since discovered by impartial observers, ☞ that the master race of this continent is found in the Southern States. ☜ Of a better stock originally, they have ruled in affairs of State by force of the stronger will and larger wisdom. ☞ This natural dominiancy of the Southern people had much to do in bringing on this war; with us the contest is for hereditary right, for the old repute of better blood." ☜

At a meeting, held in Baltimore, April, 1863, the following among other resolutions were, after grave discussion, passed by the ablest men and largest slaveholders of the State: "Resolved, that the origin and progress of the rebellion leave no room to doubt that the institution of slavery has become an instrument in the hands of ☞ traitors to build an oligarchy ☜ and an aristocracy on the ruins of Republican liberty."

In the "Richmond Examiner," may be found the following language: "We have got to hating every thing with the prefix "free," free farms, free labor, free children, ☞ but the worst of all these abominations is free schools, they belong to the same brood of damnable isms whose mother is sin and whose daddy is the devil."

The "Musiogee Herald," published in Alabama, says, in regard to free society. "We sicken at the name; what is it but a conglomeration of greasy mechanics, filthy operatives, small fisted farmers, and moon-struck theorists; all the Northern States are devoid of well-bred gentlemen; the prevailing class one meets with is that of mechanics struggling to be genteel, and small farmers, who do their own drudgery, ☞ and yet are hardly fit to associate with a Southern gentleman's body servant." ☜

The "Atlanta Intelligencer," of the 20th January, 1862, says: ☞ We are fighting this war for Southern Independence and for a government of Southern States, recognizing African Slavery ☜ as an institution ordained by God, beneficial to mankind, a necessity in our social and political relations as States and in our intercourse with all other nations or States; hence the admission of any free State into our Union is not only repugnant to us, but it will be only a continuance of that evil which has brought on the war, ☞ and which we are now fighting to get rid of." ☜

We will now close under this head with one more quotation from the "Louisville Courier," once the organ of the Breckinridge Democracy of Kentucky. "As our Norman kinsmen in England, always a minority, have ruled their Saxon countrymen in political vassalage up to the present day, ☞ so have we, the Slave Oligarchs, ☜ governed the Yankees till within twelve months; we framed the constitution, for seventy years moulded the policy of the Government, and placed our own men ☞ or Northern men with Southern principles ☜ in power. On the 6th November, 1860, the Puritans emancipated themselves, and are now in violent insurrection against their former owners. A few more Bull Run thrashings ☞ will bring them under the yoke as docile as our Ethiopian chattels."

We will now consider the "Rebellion as presented under Mr. Lincoln's Administration," the difficulties with which he has been surrounded, and the policy adopted for subduing the rebels.

Ques.—Was Mr. Lincoln elected by the popular vote?

Ans.—We will give the vote of Mr. Lincoln and Mr. Douglas, they receiving the highest number cast.

Mr. Lincoln's vote was	1,857,610
Mr. Douglas " "	1,365,976
Lincoln over Douglas	491,634

Of the electoral votes cast, Mr. Lincoln's majority over Douglas, Breckinridge and Bell, was 57.

Ques.—What was the condition of Buchanan's Cabinet and both houses of Congress at the time of Mr. Lincoln's election?

Ans.—The New York World of June, 1862, will inform you. It says: "In the dark days of 1860, we had the imbecile and false-hearted Buchanan at the head of the Government; the incompetent and perfidious Cobb was ruining the public credit. The thief Floyd was transferring the public arms to the Southern States, that thorough-paced rascal Thompson was the active coadjutor of the before mentioned worthies. The Senate was presided over by the traitor Breckinridge, and both houses of Congress swarmed with secessionists."

Ques.—What were the views and feelings of Mr. Lincoln in regard to the difficulties with which he was surrounded?

Ans.—When Mr. Lincoln left Springfield for Washington, in Feb., 1861, he bade adieu to his friends and neighbors in the following language: "My friends, no one not in my situation can appreciate my feelings of sadness at this parting. To this place and the kindness of this people I owe everything. Here I have lived a quarter of a century and have passed from a young to an old man; here my children were born, and one lies buried. I now leave, not knowing when or whether ever I may return, with a task before me greater than that which rested upon the shoulders of Washington. Without the aid of that Divine Being who controls mine and all our destinies, I cannot succeed; with that assistance, I cannot fail. Trusting in him who can go with me and remain with you and be every where for good, let us confidently hope that all will yet be well."

Mr. Lincoln, while on his way to Washington, stopped at Columbus, Ohio, and in reply to Lieut. Gov. Kirk, the presiding officer of the Senate, spoke as follows, to both branches of the Legislature who were in joint session: "It is true, as has been said by the President of the Senate, that very grave responsibilities rest upon me, to which the votes of the American people have called me. I am deeply sensible of that weighty responsibility that has fallen upon me, and so feeling I cannot but turn and look for that support without which it will be impossible for me to perform that great task. I turn then and look to the American people, and to that God who has never forsaken them. Allusion has been made to the interest felt in the policy of the new administration. In the varying and repeatedly shifting scenes of the present, without a precedent which could enable us to judge by the past, it has seemed fitting that before speaking upon the difficulties of the country, ☞ I should have gained a view of the whole field, to be sure after all, being at liberty to modify and change the course of policy as future events make a change necessary."

Ques—What was the condition of the Army and Navy?

Ans.—Ex-President Buchanan said, in a letter published in the "National Intelligencer," November, 1862: "That the whole of the American army at the close of his Administration consisted of only sixteen thousand men, and as late as the same 4th of March, 1861, the time of Mr. Lincoln's inauguration, a force of not more than six hundred and fifty-three men rank and file could be mustered in Washington, and to make up this number, even the sappers and miners were brought from West Point."

Hon. Gideon Wells, Secretary of the Navy, in his report of December 1st, 1862, makes the following statement: When I entered upon the discharge of my public duties as the head of this Department, in March, 1861, there were but forty-two vessels in commission, and as stated in my last report but seventy-six vessels then attached to the Navy. Most of those in commission were abroad, and the seven hundred seamen in the pay of the Government. There were on the 10th of March, 1861, but two thousand and seven men in all the ports and receiving ships on the Atlantic coast to man our ships and protect the navy yards and depots, or to aid in suppressing the rising insurrection. Neither the expiring Administration nor Congress which had been in session until the 4th of March, 1861, had taken measures to increase or strengthen our naval power, notwithstanding the lowering aspect of public affairs, so that when a few weeks after the inauguration I desired troops for the protection of the public property at Norfolk and Annapolis, or sailors to man and remove the vessels, neither soldiers nor sailors could be procured, nor were the few ships at our yard in a condition to be put into immediate service."

Ques.—What was the condition of the rebel army and the number of arms at their disposal at this time?

Ans.—As early as February, 1861, Governor Pickens of South Carolina, stated in a message to the State Legislature, "That all possible exertions have been made to put the sea coast in a good state of defense; the goods required for the different ports are being sent forward with all possible dispatch, and arms have been put in the hands of cavalry companies formed in the parishes bordering on the sea coast."

Wigfall in a letter to a friend in Washington, April, 1861, says, in great confidence, that the Confederate army will capture Washington before the middle of June. *He says, they have one hundred thousand well armed troops*, and in less than two weeks will be on their way to Washington, and expect to winter in Philadelphia."

The "Memphis Avalanche," of May, 1861, says: "Twenty thousand soldiers are ready to march from Tennessee and Arkansas, to Columbus, Kentucky, so hurry up your battery at Columbus, gallant men of Western Kentucky, who we know are sound to a man in the cause of Southern rights; Tennessee and Arkansas will be with you in the fight; *just say how many troops you want and you shall have them.*"

The "Memphis Appeal," of May, 1861, makes the following statement in regard to arms in the South; "The erroneous opinion seems prevalent in some quarters, that the South is totally destitute of arms. An estimate of the amount on hand, however, *will show our state of preparation for resistance.* The following seizures have been made since the Southern movement:

Baton Rouge,	70,000	Charleston,	23,000
Alabama Arsenel,	20,000	Harper's Ferry,	5,000
Elizabeth, N. C.,	30,000	Norfolk,	7,000
Fayettville, N. C.,	35,000	Other Places,	100,000
			290,000

The State arms previously purchased by the States:

Alabama,	80,000	South Carolina,	120,000
Virginia,	73,000	Mississippi,	50,000
Louisiana,	30,000	Florida,	17,000
Georgia,	120,000		
			417,000
			290,000
			707,000

The grand total *amounting to seven hundred and seven thousand stand of arms*, besides 200,000 revolvers which are on hand at other points. We have not included in the above, the arms owned by the States of Tennessee, Arkansas, Texas, Kentucky, Maryland, and Virginia."

Ques.—Is it possible that such great preparations were made under Buchanan's Administration, and the country kept in ignorance of the fact?

Ans.—Such is the case. A few leaders of the rebellion at Washington and in the South, were secretly laying out the work, while the masses were ignorant of their plans.

Ques.—Can we not, under all these circumstances, see the propriety of the remarks of Mr. Lincoln to the citizens of Bufialo, when on his way to Washington, and before his inauguration? "Your worthy Mayor has thought fit to express the hope that I may bee able to relieve the country from existing difficuulties. *I am sure I bring a true heart to the work.* When we speak of threatened difficulties, it is natural that something should be said by myself in regard to particular measures, upon more mature reflection, however others will agree with me that these difficulties are without precedent, and have never, been acted upon by any individual situated as I am. ☞ It is meet that I should wait and see the developments, and get all the light possible, so that when I do speak authoritatively, I may be as near right as possible. ☜

Ques.—What was one of the first important acts of Mr. Lincoln after his inauguration?

Ans.—He notified the Governor of South Carolina, that an attempt would be made to send provisions to Major Anderson, and the brave soldiers who were in Fort Sumter, and if there was no resistance offered, then there would be no attempt to throw in men and arms, or ammunition, without further notice, or in case of an attack upon the Fort, and furthermore, *Mr. Lincoln said*, "*you can have no conflict without you yourselves are the aggressors.*"

Ques.—Were those brave men permitted to receive provisions?

Ans.—They were not; as soon as it was telegraphed to the rebel Government that ships with provisions had sailed from New York, they determined that supplies should not be thrown into Fort Sumter. At twenty minutes past 4 o'clock, Friday morning, April 13, 1861, the bombardment commenced against Fort Sumter, from the rebel batteries of Fort Moultrie, Fort Johnson, Cumming's Point and Stevens' Battery. Fort Sumter was several times set on fire by the red hot shot from Fort Moultrie, the officers' quarters had ignited, and the flames raged fiercely. The little garrison worked with energy in repelling an enemy without and subduing a fiercer one within; by noon all the buildings were on fire, and to add to the frightful scene, there were several explosions of magazines, a raft was hastily constructed and laden with men who passed up buckets of water to their comrades in the fort in a vain attempt to extinguish the flames. During this time the Federal flag was displayed at half mast as a signal of distress, still the iron hail poured out remorselessly and incessantly from the confederate batteries; yet the most devoted loyalty to their flag, animated that handful of brave hearts, thus hopelessly battling against such overwhelming odds. After struggling against such fearful odds for forty hours, Major Anderson felt the necessity of raising a flag of truce:"

Ques.—How soon after the fall of Sumter did Mr. Lincoln call for seventy-five thousand troops?

Ans.—The next day, April 15, 1861, and on the 18th, the first troops arrived in Washington.

Ques.—Was there not in Washington at this time many rebel spies and traitors?

Ans.—There was, not only at Washington, but throughout the North.

Ques.—Was it not necessary, under these circumstances to suspend the privilege of the writ of "habeas corpus?"

Ans.—The revolution going on in the South, and there being many in the North assisting the rebels, rendered it necessary that it should be done.

Ques.—What did Mr. Lincoln say, upon the subject in his message to Congress, 4th July, 1861?

Ans.—"Soon after the first call for militia, it was considered a duty to authorize the commanding general in proper cases, according to his discretion, to suspend the privilege of the habeas corpus, or in other words to arrest and detain without resort to ordinary process and forms of law, such individuals as he might deem dangerous to the public safety. Now it is insisted that Congress, and not the executive, is invested with this power, but the Constitution itself is silent as to which or who is to usurp the power, and as the provision was plainly made for a dangerous emergency, it cannot be believed that the framers of the instrument intended that in every case the danger should run its course until Congress should be called together, the very assembling of which might be prevented, *as was intended in this case by the rebellion.*"

Ques.—Has not Mr. Lincoln been charged with committing an act not warranted by the Constitution or any former precedent?

Ans.—The enemies of Mr. Lincoln so condemn him, but the day is not far distant when he will be sustained by an American people.

Ques.—Have we other instances upon record bearing upon this subject?

Ans.—There are; to which we call your attention:

In 1777, twenty gentlemen of high respectability in the city of Philadelphia, were arrested by order of the Supreme Council of Pennsylvania, banished to a town in Virginia, and there detained. These arrests were made with the knowledge and approbation of Gen. Washington. A writ of *habeas corpus* was issued, but it was disregarded by the officers in charge of them. September 16, 1777, the Legislature passed a bill indemnifying the Executive Council and suspending the writ of *habeas corpus.*

In 1806, Gen. Wilkinson caused the arrest of certain traitors in New Orleans, implicated in Burr's conspiracy. Judge Workman of that city issued a writ of *habeas corpus* in the case, but it was disregarded. President Jefferson used the following language in regard to the matter: "A strict observance of the written law is doubtless one of the high duties of a good citizen, ☞ but it is not the highest; the laws of necessity of self-preservation, of saving our country when in danger, ARE ALL OF HIGHER OBLIGATIONS."

In the celebrated speech of Stephen A. Douglas, of January 10, 1844, in regard to the suspension of the writ of *habeas corpus*, may be found the following language: "If his (Gen Jackson's) acts were necessary to the defense of the country, THAT NECESSITY WAS ABOVE ALL LAW, and the man that dared do that, deserved the protection and plaudits of his country. He did not envy the feelings of that man who could get up and talk calmly and coolly under cuch circumstances about rules of court and formalities of proceedings. ☞ The man that would do this would fiddle while the Capital was burning. Talk about formalities; why there was but one formality to be observed, and that was the formality of directing the cannon and destroying the enemy regardless of means, WHETHER IT BE BY THE SEIZURE OF PERSONS if the necessity of the case require it, to defend the country, let him not be told that it was unconstitutional to use the necessary means. If Martial Law was necessary for the salvation of the country, Martial Law was legal for that purpose. If it was necessary for a Judge for the preservation of order to punish for contempt, he, thought it was necessary for a General to exercise control over his cannon, to impress traitors and to arrest spies, and to intercept communication with the enemy—if this WAS NECESSARY, THIS WAS LEGAL."

Ques.—Did Congress sustain Mr Lincoln in suspending the writ of habeas corpus?

Ans.—The Senate and House of Representatives, by a statute which was approved on the 3d day of March, 1863, "authorized the President to suspend the privilege of the writ of habeas corpus whenever in his judgment the public safety may require it, in any State throughout the United States."

Ques.—What other important acts have been passed under Mr. Lincoln's administration?

Ans.—The Conscription Act, the Emancipation Proclamation, Confiscation Act, and organization of Negro regiments.

Ques.—When was the Confiscation Act passed?

Ans.—Congress passed the act the 17th July, 1862.

Ques.—Were not the rebels given sixty days (after due notice by the President) to return to their allegiance to the United States, before their property would be confiscated?

Ans.—That was the order of Congress; and in accordance therewith the President gave due and timely warning, on the 25th of the same month.

Ques.—Who, then, is to blame if their property was taken from them?

Ans.—No others but themselves, and the unanimous verdict of the people in the North was, that it was just and right.

The New York *World* (Conservative) said: "For ourselves we approve the Confiscation Act, and see nothing which should change our opinion."

Ques.—How has the Emancipation Proclamation been received by the people in the loyal States?

Ans.—All true and loyal men have indorsed it, while the Anti-War, Tory Conservaive Democracy have denounced it, although some of these approved it at first.

Ques. When was the Proclamation issued?

Ans. On the 22d day of September, 1862.

Ques. What length of time did it run before taking effect?

Ans. About one hundred days, or until the 1st of January, 1863.

Ques. Had not the rebels sufficient time and opportunity to accept of the proffered terms?

Ans. They certainly had, but they were determined not to accept of any overtures of mercy, as Wigfall and Pryor made their boasts in Washington, just before the inauguration of the rebellion, ☞ "that if the entire North would put their signatures to a blank piece of paper, allowing the South to fill it up over their names and dictate the terms on which they would stay in the Union, they would not accept it, because they wanted to go out and have an independent Government of their own."

Ques. Had Mr. Lincoln the power to enforce such a law?

Ans. The President being Commander-in-chief of the army and navy in time of actual armed rebellion against the authority of the Government of the United States, did so, as a fit and necessary war measure for suppressing said rebellion, at the same time giving the rebels ample time to reflect and return to their allegiance to the United States

Ques. Did the Proclamation extend to all the States wherein slavery existed?

Ans. It only extended to those States that were in actual and armed rebellion and continued so until the 1st of January, 1863.

Ques. What evidence of approval of the Proclamation have we? and the consequences of secession?

Ans. Abundant testimony can be produced. We call your attention to a few instances.

The "New York World" used the following language: "Emancipation was a risk the South consented to incur when they joined the rebellion. We have no commiseration to waste upon them, and they are weaklings and cravens if they whine over the foreseen consequences of their own acts."

The "Kent News," of May, 1862, published in Maryland, says: "But for secession we should yet have been peaceful and prosperous. To it we trace all the evils we are now laboring under, and on the heads of the secessionists of Maryland equally with those of the South Carolina leaders, must rest all the responsibility of high taxes, depreciation of property and *abolition of slavery.*"

Gov. Hicks, of Maryland, in a speech, said: "If slavery stands in the way, let it go. I am a slaveholder, but my principles are, my country first, last, and all the time!"

In a speech against secession in the South Carolina Legislature, three years ago, Mr. Boyce of that State uttered these prophetic words: "I object in as strong terms as I can, to the secession of South Carolina. Such is the intensity of my convictions upon the subject, that if secession should take place—of which I have no idea, for I cannot believe in the existence of such a stupendous madness—I SHALL CONSIDER THE INSTITUTION OF SLAVERY AS DOOMED, and that the great God in our blindness has made us the instrument of its destruction!"

The "Cambridge Democrat," a leading Maryland journal, says: "What he (the President) or his party will next do or sanction, we know not. Certain it is his emancipation acts are meeting with response in Maryland."

Hon. Joseph Holt, of Kentucky, says: "No one can doubt the power of Mr. Lincoln to issue a proclamation of emancipation."

The following is an extract from a letter written by a resident of Georgia in July, 1863: ☞ "The Emancipation Proclamation of Mr. Lincoln struck Jeff. Davis the hardest blow he has received."

At a large meeting held at the Cooper Institute, New York City, October, 1862, the following resolution was passed unanimously:

"*Resolved,* That we regard the Confiscation Act and Emancipation Proclamation as eminently just and constitutional measures, which should be strictly enforced."

Ques. Did Mr. Lincoln adopt this policy hastily and without much study?

Ans. Mr. Lincoln said to the Rev. W. W. Patton and Rev. John Dempster, who presented a memorial to him upon that subject, from a large meeting that was held in Chicago, composed of men from the bench, from the counter, from the work-shop, from the pulpit, and men who had been warm supporters of Mr. Douglas in his contests: "The subject of emancipation occupied his mind by day and by night, and was brought renewedly to his attention by the course of events and by the arguments addressed to him. On one

: or the other he wanted to be satisfied, before issuing a proclamation of Freedom, it ıld not be a *brutum fulmen;* that it would readily accomplish its end in strengthening cause of the Union and giving liberty to the slave. He was anxious to know the will Providence in the matter; if he could find out what it was, he felt sure, unless he was ssly self-deceived, that he would do it."

At a meeting of the Governors of the loyal States, held at Altoona, Pa., September 1862, the following is a part of an address to the President of the United States:

"We hail with heartfelt gratitude and encouraged hope, the Proclamation of the sident, issued on the 22d of September, declaring emancipated from bondage all pers held to service or labor as slaves, in the rebel States, whose rebellion shall last until 1st day of January." [Signed]

G. Curtin,	Governor of	Pennsylvania,	O. P. Morton,	Governor of	Indiana,
A. Andrew,	"	Mass.,	Wm. Sprague,	"	R'd Island,
ich. Yates,	"	Illinois,	F. H. Pierpont,	"	W. Virginia,
Washburn,	"	Maine,	David Tod,	"	Ohio,
E. Salomon,	"	Wisconsin,	U. S. Berry,	"	Vermont,
J. Kirkwood,	"	Iowa,	Austin Blair,	"	Michigan.

Ques. What is understood by the Conscription Act?

Ans. A bill that was passed by Congress, February 26th, 1863, for drafting soldiers the army.

Ques. Had not this policy been urged upon the Government?

Ans. It had, from many parts of the country. Many of the Democratic papers urged draft. The "New York World," of July, 1862, used the following language: "The for volunteers under the present circumstances, will not accomplish the end; there o other way but to resort to drafting, and the sooner this is done the better. Let the ernment not hesitate a single week. We must reinforce, and there is no way to reine with sufficient promptitude except by drafting."

ı August the same paper says: "Many men dread a resort to drafting, but a general t, one which should raise half a million instead of three hundred thousand, would be eat benefit, as it is the only means which can insure the putting down of the rebellion. ; result may, by a fortunate train of circumstances, be attained by the numbers that be secured by volunteering, yet it is all uncertain. The only safe reliance is in the ıly which only drafting can yield."

The "Illinois State Register," of August, 1862, said: "We are in favor of drafting, ;use this is a terrible war on our hands, and soldiers will not come voluntarily; thouls and tens of thousands will volunteer rather than be drafted, but there are many 3 tens of thousands who will have to be forced in."

The "Albany Atlas and Argus," spoke repeatedly to the same purpose, on the 11th uly, 1862, urged Congress to pass a conscription act before adjourning. On the 31st uly, it used the following language: "No war of proportions like the present was ever lucted by volunteering. Throughout all Europe, conscription is the rule." On the 5th of August, the same paper said: "The demand upon the State has been greater than ever dreamed of by the wildest imagination. It has been met with wonderful alacrity facility; it is now doubled, and the exigencies of the occasion demands a draft."

The "Dubuque Herald," of July, 1862, said: "The fairest way to raise troops is by ing, for it is the only way that those who have been the principal cause of the existvar, can be made to bear their share of its sacrifices and hardships."

ıe "Boston Daily Advertiser," says: In spite of the occasional attempts of the ultra sition to represent the conscription bill as a despotic, and cruel measure, the majority ır people will have no regret at its passage, except that it was not passed a year er."

Ques. Was the organization of Negro regiments a wise policy?

Ans. It certainly was. Many negroes were anxious to enlist into the Union army. hundred thousand have already been mustered into the service; they have proved selves good soldiers, and every one enlisted saves that many white soldiers.

Ques. Were they not admitted into the rebel service a long time before mustered the Union army?

Ans. On the 2d of Feb., 1861, Fort Palmetto, on Cole Island, in the harbor of South lina, was completed, and the soldiers then celebrated the event by raising the Palmetg. Some fifty Negroes who had assisted in digging ditches, the Mercury says then assembled on the ramparts around the flag staff and gave utterance to the following s timents: "We are de fust dat come to dis fort, we work on 'em til'e finish, tree chairs Palmetto flag, tree chairs for Capen Poff. and tree more for Sous Carolina."

The "Memphis Appeal," and "Memphis Avalanche," of May 9th, 10th, and 1 1861, had the following notice: "Attention, volunteers! Resolved, by the committe safety, that C. Deloach, D. R. Cook and W. B. Greenlaw be authorized to organize a c pany comprised of free men of color of the City of Memphis, for the service of our c mon defense. All who have not enrolled their names will call at the office of Wm. Greenlaw & Co."

The "Mobile Register," says: "That the Negro is no longer an object of small t in the South. The people in the South have a place for them, and that is in the arn

Ques. Were black men used as soldiers in the Revolutionary war, and the wa 1812?

Ans. Mr. Livermore, who has collected much evidence on this point, says: "At battle of Bunker Hill, 17th of June, 1775, negro soldiers stood side by side and fou bravely with their white brethren, and Peter Salem, a negro soldier once a slave, fired shot which killed Major Pitcain, of the British Marines, who led the assault."

In 1776, Gen. Green reports to Washington, that 800 Negroes were then collecte Staten Island to be formed into a regiment. On the 23d of October, 1777, a Hessian ficer who was with Burgoyne at the time of his surrender, wrote in his journal. of army: "The Negro can take the field instead of his master, and therefore no regimen to be seen in which there are not Negroes in abundance, and among them are able bod strong and brave soldiers."

When Col. Green was surprised, and murdered near Points Bridge, New York, on 14th of May, 1781, his colored soldiers heroically defended him till they were cut to pie and the enemy reached him over the dead bodies of his faithful Negroes.

Mr. Madison thought it advisable to enlist blacks; so also did Gen. Washington, wrote a letter to that effect in December, 1775.

Early in 1778, it was proposed by Gen. Barnum to Washington, that the two Rl Island battalions in camp at Valley Forge should be united, and that the officers of Col. Green, Lieut. Col. Olney, and Major Ward, with their subalterns, be sent to Rhod land to enlist a battalion of Negroes, for the continental service; this plan was appro and the officers were sent home for that purpose.

In Virginia an act was past, emancipating all slaves who had served their ter the army faithfully. The act acknowledged that such persons having contributed tow the establishment of American liberty and independence, should enjoy the blessin freedom, as a reward for their toils and labors.

The following address of Gen. Jackson was read to the black soldiers in New leans, Dec. 18th, 1814: "Soldiers from the shores of Mobile, I collected you to arr invited you to share in the perils, and to divide the glory of your white countrymen; pected much from you, for I was not uninformed of those qualities which must render so formidable to an invading foe. I knew that you could endure hunger and thirst, all the hardships of war; I knew that you loved the land of your nativity, and that ourselves you had to defend all that is most dear to man, but you surpass my hop have found in you, united to those qualities, that noble enthusiam which impels to g deeds."

Ques. Why is it, with our large army and navy, the vast resources of the cou the great preparations that have been made, and are still making for the success o Federal arms and the salvation of our country, that the rebellion has not long since subdued, and peace and quiet again restored to our once happy, but now distracted c try?

Ans. Two reasons will be given to the above question: 1st, a negative, or wha not been the reason; 2d, a positive answer, or show by facts wherein the difficulty e and who are to blame.

1st, negatively. The fault cannot be imputed to Mr. Lincoln, as he said befor inauguration, "he brought an honest heart to the work," which statement has bee emplified throughout his whole course. He said to the South, ☞ "you yourselves not have war without you being the aggressors." ☜

In April, 1861, he calls upon those who were in open rebellion against the Go ment, to lay down their arms, and return to their respective callings; and thereby pr all the horrors of a civil war.

In July, 1862, he issued another proclamation, calling upon those who were in open lion to the Government, to return to their allegiance to the United States, giving them days to consider the matter, and in case of refusal their property would be confis- l.

In Sept., 1862, he issued another proclamation to the rebels, to return to their allegi- to the Government' giving them one hundred days to meditate upon the subject, and ıse of refusal at the end of that time, their slaves should be emancipated.

In Dec., 1863, he issued another proclamation, holding out the olive branch to the s, and saying to them, that a full pardon would be granted to all those below the of Colonel, if they would lay down their arms, and swear to be good and loyal sub- of the Government. Well may Mr. Lincoln say, what more can I do? "I have d and ye have refused, I have stretched out my hand and ye have not regarded it."

Neither was it because Mr. Lincoln was not the right man in the right place.

The "New York World," of March, 1862, in speaking of Mr. Lincoln's character, "We have had many Presidents who could reach decisions more rapidly, but none, ven Jackson, whose mind was more self-determined. Take the most important acts s administration, and see how perfectly they bear the impress of his unassisted hand. to this unborrowed strength of character, combined ☞ with perfect honesty, ☜ the country has the best of guarantee for the preservation of our institutions."

The "London Spectator," one of the most respectable journals of Europe, says, "Mr. oln has been tested as few Presidents have ever been tested, and though he may not ys have been fully to the level of a great emergency, he has seldom failed to display ole impartiality, a great firmness of purpose, and a sagacious, if somewhat utilitarian nent. We believe a juster man never held the reigns of Government."

The "Staats Zeitung," says, in regard to Mr. Lincoln, "Always in sympathy with the ıct of the American masses, from whose ranks he came, the President has advanced position to position, slowly indeed, so that the laggard foot, and the heart full of oding, could follow him but surely and steadily; and he has in no instance taken a backward: to the convictions that have been forced upon him by the logic of events, iis own not rapid, but clear and sharp comprehension, he has clung with unwavering ty; and what he perceives to be right, that he does without timidity, though perhaps a certain moderation which has its origin in the goodness of his nature. So the es not incorrectly judge of him, and hence it follows that spite of the enormous sac- s which he has hitherto called for, and is still expecting from the American people, pite of the endless difficulties of his situation, *he is still, after an administration of -three months, the most popular man in the nation.*"

Neither has the want of our success been owing to a lack of courage on the part of rmies. The land is filled with mourning for those who have fallen at the battles of Bethel, Rich Mountain, Balls Bluff, Fort Donelson, Shiloh, Columbus, Island No. 10, burg, Pea Ridge, Port Hudson, Fredericksburg, Gettysburg, Stone River, Chicka- a and many other places.

We will now offer three principal reasons why the rebellion has not long since been ed:

st. The real strength of the South has been under-estimated.

nd. The hopes of Foreign Intervention have encouraged the rebels to hold on; and

rd. The aid and encouragement the rebels have received from the anti-War, Tory, rvative democrats, have been productive of more evil than all other causes com-

We will refer to the first two reasons briefly, but upon the last we will show by good ıfficient testimony which shall be from themselves, and the South shall bear testi- also, and all loyal Americans shall be the judges and decide if the charges have een fully sustained.

Ques. How has the real strength of the South been under-estimated?

Ans. By not including the blacks, as every one used by them is considered equal to hite man.

Ques. Has the South made this statement?

Ans. The "Richmond Whig" enumerates the Southern strength of whites between es of fifteen and fifty, to be two millions; this force can be kept in the field as long North may assail us, and will not interfere with our agricultural population; our can be safely trusted to the management of the boys under eighteen years, and the en, *and abundant crops be thus secured while our fighting men are in the field.*

Not so with the North; whenever she puts anything like her military strength in the she weakens her power to feed her people; and though her white population in 1860 19,000,000, against 8,700,000 whites in the South, and though she ought, therefore, able to send out two soldiers where we can send one, yet we question much if sh send out her one million as readily as the South can."

Ques. Have the South made strong efforts for Foreign Intervention?

Ans. They have, as the following testimony will show:

In May, 1861, Lord Russell reports to Lord Lyons, the substance of a convers he held with Messrs. Yancey, Rost and Mann, delegates from the Confederate States

FOREIGN OFFICE, May 11, 1

MY LORD: "On Saturday last, I received at my house, Mr. Yancey, Mr. Mann and Rost, the three gentlemen deputed by the Southern Confederacy, to obtain their recog as an Independent State; one of these gentlemen, speaking for the others, dilated c causes which had induced the Southern States to secede from the Northern; *the princ these causes, he said, was not slavery,* but the very high prices which for the sake of prot to the Northern manufactures, the South were obliged to pay for the manufactured which they required. I said I could hold no official communication with the delegates c Southern States; that, however, when the question of recognition came to be formall cussed, there were two points upon which inquiry must be made: First, whether the seeking recognition could maintain its position as an independent State; Secondly, In manner it was proposed to maintain relations with Foreign States. After speaking at length on the first of these points, and alluding to the secession of Virginia, and other ligence favorable to the cause concluded by stating that they should remain in London, f present, in the hope that the recognition of the Southern Confederacy would not be lo layed."

These Commissioners could not get Lord Russell "to see it." And after waitin watching, they learn that other Commissioners will be sent from the rebel Government. Accordingly two noted Tories, Mason and Slidell, were sent, November, 1861, (in a E vessel, "Trent,") as Commissioners to treat with England for the establishment of a Sou Confederacy; they secured the co-operation of the London Times, also the services of le men in England and France, were obtained to advocate the Southern cause. Vessel fitted out in England for the Southern Confederacy; sensation articles were published in don journals in order to strengthen the South, and after two years of painful anxiet North and South, as to the course England would take, Mason dispels all doubts, by w a doleful letter to Earl Russell, dated London, September 21st, 1863:

MY LORD: In a dispatch from the Secretary of State of the Confederate States of ica, dated 4th of August last, and now just received, I am instructed to consider the n which brought me to England, as at an end, and I am directed to withdraw at once fro country. The reasons for terminating this mission are set forth in an extract from th patch, which I have the honor to communicate herewith. "The President believes th Government of her Majesty has determined to decline the overtures made through you tablishing by treaty, friendly relations between the two governments, and entertai intention of receiving you as the accredited Minister of this government near the I Court. Under these circumstances, your continued residence in London is neither co ive to the interests, nor consistent with the dignity of this government, and the Pre therefore requests that you consider your mission at an end, and that you withdraw wit Secretary from London." Having made known to your lordship, on my arrival he character and purposes of the mission intrusted to me by my government, I have dee due to courtesy, thus to make known to the government of Her Majesty, its terminatio that I shall, as directed, at once withdraw from England.

I have the honor to be, your Lordship's very obedient servant,

J. M. MASO

Ques. How is it, that the course the Anti-War Conservative Democrats have has been productive of more evil than all other causes combined?

Ans. By their opposition to the Government, and giving aid and comfort to bels.

Ques. What is their record, and how has it been received by the rebels?

RECORD OF THE ANTI-WAR CONSERVATIVE DEMOCRATS.

At a meeting of the Democratic Central Committee, of the City of Chicago, May 25th,

RECORD OF THE REBELS IN THE SOU

The Chattanooga "Rebel," in an e of May 29th, 1863, says, in regard Vallandigham, "How natural it is

;, the following resolutions were unani-
sly adopted:

'HEREAS, The Hon. C. L. Vallandigham,
:izen of the State of Ohio, has been ar-
ed without the intervention of jury, and
lemned to banishment, for exercising his
stitutional right of free speech; and,

'HEREAS, The President, Abraham Lin-
, by his approval thereof, has clearly in-
ted that it is the intention of this Admin-
ition to subvert the liberties of the peo-
and erect a military despotism upon the
is of the Republic; therefore be it

esolved, That the Democratic Central
imittee of the State of Illinois are rested to call a convention of the Democra-
nd other citizens of this State, (or of the
th Western States,) who are determined
naintain all their constitutional rights,
neet at some early day, to vindicate the
ts of free speech, and consult as to the
sures necessary for their common safety.

esolved, That in the name of ten thousand
rs of Chicago, we tender to Governor Sey-
r of the State of New York, our heartfelt
ks for his noble and patriotic letter to
e late free speech meeting at the city of
ny.

1e "Chicago Times," (the organ for the
-War Tory, Conservative Democrats,)
eaking of Vallandigham, in July, 1863,

Ir. Vallandigham should not wait any
ission of the President to return; he
d return of his own will and pleasure.
said to have left the Confederacy on his
o some one of the British Colonial ports,
lockade runner, his only means of escape.
ould, as his right, boldly in the light of
come back to Ohio. If the Federal mil-
authorities attempt to interfere with him,
e Democracy of Ohio take care of him.
ever he shall enter the United States,
nnot doubt that he will have an escort
usands; and when he shall enter Ohio,
ll be received as a man in the country
ver been received before."

"Chicago Times," of April, 1862,
"It is worse than folly to talk of co-
the Southern States into submission
Federal Government. It would be
sible to accomplish such a result, and
f it were not, such a policy would be
ost disastrous in every respect, that
possibly be pursued."
can tell the Republican party every-
one thing, that if the refusal to re-
ie personal liberty laws shall be per-
n; and if there shall be no change
present seeming purpose to yield to
ommodation of the National difficul-
d if troops shall be raised in the
o march against the people of the
☞ a fire in the rear will be opened
ich troops which will either stop their

all feel kindly towards Mr. Vallandigham; we do not doubt the course he will adopt, we really consider his prospects to be Governor of Ohio very fair; we wish them realized because he is a peace man, an able and honest one. *He is our style of man*, and as such we do not wish him consigned to the obscurity and misfortunes of an exile, when he is powerful for good. While he is with us, let us show him how deeply we can sympathize with a foeman worthy of our steel, a generous enemy.

"*We admire McClellan, and we admire Buell also*, we admire Mr. Vallandigham more than all because he was against the war at the start and has kept his faith ever since."

On the 29th, the same paper says, "His, (Vallandigham's,) road which leads up the steep ascent of the future, is direct and gas-lighted all the way; it leads first out of some Confederate port to Nassau; thence to Canada, and finally to the Gubernatorial chair of Ohio. Let Mr. Vallandigham's return be as speedy as possible; let the absence of a single month find him issuing an address to the people of Ohio, from Lower Canada, proclaiming these things to them:

"'I, C. L. Vallandigham, a loyal citizen of the Union, persecuted, exiled, mobbed and coerced by cowardly tyrants, and by bayonets, but not dead nor dumb, issue these words, and declare myself a candidate for Governor of Ohio.'"

The Georgia "Constitutionalist," before the battle of Chickamauga, urged Bragg to strike Rosecrans a crushing blow, giving the following reasons therefor:

"We were never more fully convinced than now, of the essential importance of thick, fast and heavy blows from the Confederate armies, in order to give vitality, system and organization to the Peace men. Mr. Vallandigham himself, as we have heard, most emphatically declared, that the success of Southern arms alone could give strength and consistency to the Peace movement."

(From the Cincinnati Commercial.)

When Morgan's band was going through Ohio, they stopped at a hickory pole at New Baltimore, in Hamilton county, and hurrahed for Vallandigham; and they said, if Abe Lincoln did not let him come home, *they would bring him back to Ohio.*

The traitor, M. F. Maury, wrote a letter to the "London Times," August 17, 1863, in which he says: ☞ Vallandigham waits and watches over the border, pledged, if elected Governor of Ohio, to array it against Lincoln and the war, ☜ and go for peace." "And other agents have been called in play; what are they? let us inquire. They are divisions in the camp of the enemy, dissensions among the people march altogether, or wonderfully accelerate it."

When the blood-thirsty Irish thugs were howling, burning, plundering and murdering in New York City, July, 1863, Governor Seymour addressed them in the following language: *My noble friends*, I have sent to Washington to have the draft stopped; I will have the constitutionality of the act tested by our State Courts, and if they pronounce against the law, I'll support their decision by the whole power of the State."

At a meeting of Peace Democrats held in Chicago, December 3, 1863, the following resolution was adopted:

Resolved, That the power of the Federal Government to make war upon a sovereign State of this Union, is wholly inconsistent with, and contrary to the intentions of its authors. That whatever be the theory of constitutional power, war, as a means of restoration of the Union, is a delusion involving the waste of human life, national bankruptcy, and the downfall of the Republic.

"*That we are in favor of peace, an unconditional peace.*"

The Chicago Times, of December 12th, 1863, says, "If we have less respect for war Democrats than for Peace Democrats, it is because the former are designedly auxiliary to the abolition party, and in its immediate service, whereas the latter serve abolitionism only as they divide and distract the Democratic party. Good Democrats will have no connection with movements outside of the regular Democratic organization, whatever the professed objects of such movements may be. If the country can be saved only as it shall be saved *by the Democratic party*, as we solemnly believe, the democratic party will be potent to that end only as its unity and integrity shall be preserved. It will not permit segments to make its policies, or to lead or control it in any manner."

Major Key, who was on General Halleck's staff, by a recommendation from General McClellan, said to an officer after the battle of "Antietam," ☞ "the immediate destruction of the Rebel army was not the programme. It would be better, he said, to let the war linger on indecisively, and with advantage to both sides, until the end of Mr. Lincoln's administration, when it could be settled on a compromise which would save slavery." ☜

of the North. There is already a pea party there; ☞ all the embarrassm with which the party can surround M Lincoln, and all the difficulties that it c throw in the way of the war party in North, operate directly as so much aid a comfort to the South." ☜

The editor of the "Vicksburg Whig October, 1862, said: ☞ "All the ener of the Confederacy will be bent to main the war until the expiration of Mr. Linco presidential term; ☜ the idea has come general, that by that time, a man be elected who will represent the view the Peace Democrats. It is well ur stood that every day adds to the numb their friends, and that already *Nort secessionists, conservatives as they called here*, are in a numerical majc Every argument used in the North in r ence to the constitutional rights of m *hailed with delight.*

☞ The "Chicago Times," which i versally regarded as their great advoc the North-west, is almost entirely repr in the Southern papers; ☜ all the vention proceedings, proceedings o Peace Democrats, are immediately c and spread broadcast, and received wi wildest joy."

The Richmond Whig, says, "So fa wishing for the arrest of such men a mour and Hunt, we applaud every ef theirs which tends to embarrass Li Chase and Sumner, and weaken their *we would like to see them get posses the Government*; take the very wor of such a contingency, and we wou nothing."

The Point Coupe *Echo*, (*La.*,) a sheet, says, "The great speech of Di rick, of Illinois, will have its effect where, and will sow the seed of dis in the ranks of the Federal troops, thing will. The whole West will soo forth. We see the smoke, and fire far distant. ☞ God speed the go and let the whole puritanical North veloped in ruin and desolation." ☜

The Richmond *Examiner,* of Fe 1863, says, "Amongst the foreign r of the Confederacy, none is at this more interesting than *our relatio the States of Indiana and Illi* represents to us every day, and we to be a fact that the people of thos

Vhen the Democratic convention was in sion in Springfield, Illinois, Wednesday, ie 15, 1864, a telegram was received from o, saying that Vallandigham had re- ied from Canada, and was then address- *a Democratic convention* in Hamilton, *'ch was received with uproarious cheer-*; one of the members of the convention ed that the convention resolve to sus- C. L. Vallandigham in his rights, and d by the State of Ohio in so doing, :h was carried, *and the President was cted to telegraph the resolution to* o.

r. Green, chairman of that convention, aking his seat, returned thanks in the l style; *waxing eloquent over Lincoln otism, accumulated debt,* and disregard e Government principles instituted by Fathers of the Revolution. He coun- l them to work together in harmony. eferred in triumphant tones to the Fremont movement as a hopeful sign em; one which would enable them more to ride into power and save the ry. ☚

are heartily tired of the war as waged by the abolitionists. ☞Democrats in those States bring in strings of resolutions denouncing Lincoln's government and proclamation. This is all very well and highly encouraging to us, ☚ but it is also well for us to understand once for all, that the whole affair means simply, ☞ that they, the democrats, ought to conduct and have the profits of the war for the Union; that a democratic finance minister ought to have the striking off of "greenbacks;" democratic contractors ought to supply the Army and Navy; democratic Generals ought to lead· democratic printers ought to print, and democratic thieves ought to steal." ☚

es. Have the South desired a compromise with the North, and a return to the ı ?

s. They have not, as their record will show all the way through.

Senator Iverson, of Georgia, said, before Mr. Lincoln's inauguration: "That the intends to go out of the Union."

Pryor, of Virginia, said: "We can get the Crittenden Compromise, but we don't it."

Vigfall said: "If the North would furnish them a piece of white paper to dictate own terms on which they would stay in the Union, they would not accept it, as they determined to have a government of their own."

Leader, you will notice the above was said before Mr. Lincoln's inauguration.

'he Richmond *Whig* of 1861, says: "This war must go on. The South must fight he North sues for peace. We must dictate the terms of peace. The first article ch should be an acknowledgment of the right of secession; the next article to be ie pay the utmost farthing of the expense of this war, and the third that she pay destruction of all property, and the fourth, that she impeach and remove from Abe Lincoln, and hang him for treason and other crimes."

eff. Davis, in his Message to Congress, in April, 1861, says: "Our cause is just and We seek no conquest, no aggrandizement, *no concession* from the Free States; all is to be let alone."

he Richmond *Enquirer* of 1862, says: "The only terms which the Confederate can accept, will be the immediate recognition of the present Confederate States, e permission to the other States to elect their own destiny and to decide whether ıture shall be with the Confederate States or with the United States."

ie Augusta *Constitutionalist* of 1863, says: "The Northern politicians and people , or will not, open their eyes to the great fact that a reconstruction of the Union is *ible;* all their hopes of peace and their peace propositions, are based on reconstruc- ☞ This singular fallacy or mental delusion, ought to be completely removed by ie. We have determined to gain our independence, and we cannot with honor and ourselves listen to any proposition other than a complete and unconditional ac- dgment of that independence."

e Richmond *Dispatch* of January 10th, 1863, says: "If the whole Yankee race fall down in the dust to-morrow, *and pray us to be their masters,* WE WOULD

SPURN THEM AS SLAVES! We are fighting for SEPARATION, and we will ha IF IT COST THE LIFE OF EVERY MAN IN THE CONFEDERATE STATES!

The Richmond *Enquirer* of January, 1863, says: "On no terms whatever wi South consent to a political association with the North. There is no concession ' they can grant or human imagination can frame, which could render the idea augl intolerable to the Southern mind. ☞ When the North wants peace she can obtain *recognizing the independence of the Southern States.* Her proper mode to secur result *so desirable to her*, would be at once to withdraw her armies from Southerr and send her commissioners to this capital. NOT EVEN TO BRING ABOUT HONORABLE PEACE CAN THE SOUTH MAKE THE SLIGHTEST ADVANC THE NORTH!"

Vice-President Stephens, of the Confederate Government, stopped at Charlotte, Carolina, July 17th, 1863, and was serenaded by the citizens. In a speech to th said: "*As for reconstruction, such a thing was impossible*; such an idea must not b rated for an instant. Reconstruction would not end the war, but would produce a horrible war than that in which we are now engaged. The only terms on which w obtain permanent peace, is final and complete separation from the North. Rathe to submit to anything short of that, let us all resolve to die like men worthy of free

And now, reader, have we not shown—

1st. That there are, in fact, but two parties in the North?

2d. That the South had no just cause to rebel?

3d. What were the real designs of the South in rebelling?

4th. The rebellion as presented under Mr. Lincoln's administration?

5th. The policy adopted for suppressing the rebellion?

6th. The reason the rebellion has not long since been subdued?

7th. The rebels spurn with contempt any propositions of compromise, save th recognition of their independence?

But you ask, is there not another party in the North, of which John C. Fren the acknowledged leader?

We answer: John C. Fremont has withdrawn, and strongly recommends efforts to defeat the Democratic party.

What are the parties then in the pending election?

The Union party, including War Democrats, who will support Lincoln and Jo and the Chicago Peace Party, represented by McClellan and Pendleton.

Ques. Has George B. McClellan had the capacity or disposition to subdue bellion?

Ans. The *Richmond Whig* (Rebel) of April, 1863, says: ☞ "A review McClellan's career will show that the immense nnmber of men, and the most over ing array of field artillery that has ever been seen upon this continent, at his co an officer of enterprise and daring would hurt us solely. But he did not want to f sought merely to push us from one position to another by dint of enormous numbe

McCLELLAN BEFORE RICHMOND.

The *North American* (Philadelphia) of the 15th September, has the following st from a gentleman lately in the service of War Department. It corroborates many int already before the public with regard to the Chickahominy campaign.

That Gen. McClellan is loyal, after his own way of thinking, we do not doubt. Tha meant to put down the Rebellion, and that he used the forces placed at his command to we do not and cannot believe. No sane person not an idiot could have held idle the ov ing force commanded by Gen. McClellan from October, 1861, to March, 1862, if he h *desired* the crushing out of the Rebellion. He lay in and around Washington, hen shut up, virtually besieged, by an army not one-third so large as his own, which held t more and Ohio Railroad on his right and the Potomac on his left, confining him tc track of railroad for all his supplies; when he might have crushed the foe in a week i simply tried—nay, if he alone had not peremptorily forbidden and prevented any effc rdinates. Who *can* explain such conduct? When he has tried, let him make his next on the following:

Members of the National Union Club, Philadelphia.

ENTLEMEN:—I am in possession of your note, in which you ask me if I remember having made certain ions at the rooms of the National Union Club in January last, on my return from the Rebel lines, in l to Gen. George B. McClellan and Clement L. Vallandigham, and desiring to know if I would reiterate atement.

recollect perfectly well having made certain statements in regard to the two persons named, and in pre- of several members of the Club.

response to your inquiry if I would repeat said statement, I will answer you by saying: First, That the battle before Richmond, Virginia, in 1862, was still progressing, and immediately after Gen. llan had fallen back from before that city, in company with a friend, an officer in the Rebel service, as prevented from joining his command, in the fight in question, on account of a wound received at ttle of Seven Pines, and, being provided with a special permit from the War Department at Richmond, d the fortifications around Richmond, and advanced to a distance of about two miles north of that city, we met Col. Gayle, of the 12th Alabama (Rebel) regiment, who was a particular friend of the officer in company I was; also Lieut.-Col. Pickens, of the same regiment, with whom I had the advantage of a al acquaintance. The colonel was superintending the disinterment of a number of cases of U. S. rifles, lay buried in the ground, and in rows, the soil heaped over them as if they were graves. Four of the f rifles were already unburied when I reached the spot, and I had the (to me unpleasant) satisfaction lling some of those guns, which had already been taken out of the cases.

eard Col. Gayle say that the interment of these guns was known at the War Department (Rebel) even McClellan's retreat from before that city.

the inquiry of my friend and Dr. Kelly, of the Rebel army, from Col. Gayle, if he thought it had been d that said guns should fall into the hands of the Confederates, the Colonel answered in the affirmative ncluded by saying, "Mac's all right."

more than a hundred yards distant from this spot, Lieut.-Col. Pickens pointed out to a number of nces—two hundred and ten in number—and said he had assisted at their capture, and that, when cap- he horses belonging to said ambulances were hitched, some to trees and some to the rear of the ambul- As I was then in the employ of the United States, it was my business to gather as much information d to military matters as possible, and on my inquiry of Col. Pickens if he thought these ambulances n intended to be in the same "bargain" as the rifles, he said: "I don't see what else they should en intended for, for they were just where you see them, and the horses hitched as you see them, while t was going on right here."

ently some whisky was handed round, and we all drank a toast to "Little Mac."

ut the month of April of the same year, as I was going from Richmond to Mobile, in company with Viltz add Dr. Knood of Missouri, and Dr. Fontleroy, of Virginia, the two latter gentlemen being of l General Price's staff, we met with Brigadier-General Watson of Alabama. Gen. Watson said in my that then, or at any time after the war, he could give satisfactory proof that George B. McClellan, ederal army, at the outbreak of the Rebellion and during the preliminary arrangements for the tion of the Confederate army, had offered his services to the Confederate Government, but that as the ate Government had resolved to give rank in preference to officers formerly in the United States ser- cording to seniority of rank, they could not give to McClellan what he desired, as other officers im in seniority; and that McClellan, having become offended at this, then offered his services to d States.

ecember, 1862, I had occasion to call on Gov. Shorter, of Alabama, who was then sojourning at the le Hotel, Huntsville, Alabama. Gov. Shorter introduced me to General Watson, who was present. ral recognized me immediately. And, as the Governor resumed a conversation with another person om, I, while in conversation with the General, had occasion to refer to our trip to Mobile, and I pur- ought about the conversation in reference to General McClellan, and Gen. Watson reiterated the t he had previously made in regard to McClellan.

gard to Clement L. Vallandigham, the Ohio traitor, I will say that during his sojourn at Richmond peatedly closeted with Jeff. Davis, James A. Seddon, the Rebel Secretary of War, and Judah P. Ben- e Rebel Secretary of State.

g my visit to Richmond at that epoch, I learned from reliable rsources (rebel officials) that this tor had pledged his word to the Rebel anthorities that if the Democratic party at the North succeeded g ***their candidate*** at the next Presidential election, he would use all his influence to obtain peace sis of a recognition of the Confederate States as a ***separate and independent government.***

over, during my stay at Richmond, having called on Mr. Benjamin, the Secretary of State, with a tain an interview on business of a private character, I was told by an official in attendance at the nt of State—who of course believed me to be a loyal confederate—that it was uncertain when I could see Mr. Benjamin: and that as the visitor of Mr. Benjamin was Mr. Vallandigham, whom this led the ***Ohio refugee,*** the conference might be protracted to a late hour. On that day, although I til after the hour for transacting business at that department, I did not get to see Mr. Benjamin.

at time, divers were the rumors in private circles among the Rebels that Vallandigham had pledged the Confederate cause. Of this the War Department at Washington was informed in a report made l other government agents.

were the expectations of the Rebels during my last visit within their lines, if this Vallandigham cceeded in electing their candidate to the Presidency.

be remembered that this Vallandigham faction ***are the men who seek to elect George B. n to an office which none but loyal men should fill.***

Very respectfully, yours, &c.,

EMILE BOURLIER.

lelphia, Sept. 14, 1864.

a General, having an efficient force of 180,000 as McClellan had, be considered *nt* and *loyal*, in not taking Richmond with only 12,000 to defend it?

Let his whole management of the army, his losses, defeats, and evident concess to the Rebels of time, men, and war materials without apparent justification, together his contradictory dispatches and evidences against him before the Committee on the duct of the war, his previous effort to be commissioned by Jeff. Davis, and his popul among the rebels at the time, and especially their efforts and anxiety for his nomin for the Presidency on their own Chicago Platform, and their unbounded joy at their cess, as manifested in their defences, and by guerrillas while firing on our boats. considered, and any honest patriotic mind will have reason to believe GEO. B. McCl LAN a traitor at heart.

As to George H. Pendleton, whose sympathies and acts have been entirely wit South, and against every effort to provide for our soldiers and navy, with his hearty cc ration in making and approval of the Chicago Platform, and whose associates are known traitors, he can be relied on to sustain McClellan and the South, in all thei mands, even to the sacrifice of our army, navy, and nationality.

Must not those voting for such men necessary affiliate with Traitors?

We will now close this work by referring to a portion of Stephen A. Douglas' sp delivered in Springfield, April 25th, 1861:

"We are told because a certain party has carried a Presidential election, the the South choose to consider their liberties insecure. I had supposed it was a f mental principle of American institutions, that the will of the majority, constituti expressed, should govern. If a defeat at the ballot-box is to justify rebellion, the history of the United States may be read in the past history of Mexico. The first d every American citizen is to render obedience to the National Constitution and Most of you know I am a very good fighter in times of partizan strife, *I hope to sho all that I am an equally good patriot in the time of my country's danger. It i your* IMPERATIVE DUTY *TO THROW PARTY AND PARTY PLATFC TO THE WINDS, forget that you ever differed.* Give me a country where m dren can live in peace, and then we can have a theatre if we desire, for partisan c versy. Allow me to say to my old friends, *you will be false and unworthy of principles if you allow political defeat to convert you into traitors to your Na land.* THE SHORTEST WAY NOW TO PEACE CONSISTS IN THE *STUPENDOUS AND UNANIMOUS PREPARATIONS FOR WAR!*

And now we ask you, American citizens, in view of all these facts, what will yo "*Are you willing to swap horses while crossing the stream?*" Are you willing to new commander and crew on board the ship when in sight of port? Are you wil bend the neck and come under the yoke of your *Southern masters*, as they call them will you bend the knee and pay homage to them? We ask you in the name of ever that is dear to American citizens, what will you do? "If the Lord be God, serve h Baal, serve him." If you are Freemen, worship at the shrine of Freedom; if worship at the altar of Slavery. But you ask, what hope have we; have we no discouragements, a large debt and constantly increasing, besides suffering great lo our armies? To all of which we answer, Yes; but we ask you to open your eyes who is chargeable for much of this. We have shown you that the Anti-War, Conse party must bear the responsibility; they must meet the charge before the bar American people when the history of this rebellion is written in its true light. Th of thousands of our brave and noble soldiers who now lie buried away from fri Southern soil, cries for redress—from the "*fire-in-the-rear party.*" If our arm not have had this party to contend against, we to-day could have the proud satisfa knowing that the great Ship of State has out-ridden the angry waves, and come s port, and those who sought to dash her to pieces upon the rocks have been severe ished for their temerity, and brought to know that the Union of the States is inse now and forever.

GEORGE H. PENDLETON'S RECORD.

———o———

The following passage (says the *N. Y. Tribune*) puts Mr. Pendleton in rect antagonism with Gen. McClellan. The latter is for conciliation and comomise; but if the rebels will not hear to such terms as comport with the tional honor, then he is for coercing them into obedience to the laws. Now, ırk what Mr. Pendleton says:

"My voice to-day is for conciliation; my voice is for compromise; and it is but the ıo of the voice of my constituents. I beg you, gentlemen, who with me represent the rth-West; you who with me represent the State of Ohio; you who with me represent city of Cincinnati—beg you, gentlemen, to hear that voice. If you will not; if you l conciliation impossible; if your differences are so great, that you cannot or will not oncile them, *then gentlemen, let the Seceding States depart in peace; let them esta- ·h their Government and Empire, and work out their destiny according to the wisdom :ch God has given them.*"

August 2, 1861.—Mr. Pendleton voted against the bill "to provide increased revenue from imports, ıy the interest on the public debt," &c., when it had been amended in the Senate, and was finally passed ı the recommendation of a committee of conferences.

August 5, 1861.—Mr. Pendleton voted, with 19 others, to strike from the army bill the following sec- :—And be it further enacted, That all the acts, proclamations, and orders of the President of the United ·s, after the 4th of March, 1861, respecting the army and navy of the United States, and the calling out lating to the militia or volunteers, from the States, are hereby approved, and in all respects legalized made valid, to the same intent, and with the same effect, as if they had been issued and done under the ious express authority of the Congress of the United States."

February 25, 1862.—Mr. Pendleton voted against the bill to prohibit officers of the army from re- ing fugitive slaves to their alleged owners.

April 8, 1862.—He voted against the bill to provide internal revenue, support the Government, and he interest on the public debt. He was in a minority of 15, including such Copperheads as Kerrigan, hees and Vallandigham.

May 6, 1862.—He *dodged* a vote upon the question of a Pacific Railroad, although he was present and a few minutes before upon a contested election case, and again, June 28, he *dodged* the question.

May 28, 1862.—Mr. Pendleton, with only seventeen others, voted against the bill for imposing taxes surrectionary districts.

cember 17, 1863.—Green Clay Smith, of Kentucky, submitted the following resolution:—"Resolved, our country, and the very existence of the best Government ever instituted by man, are imperiled by the causeless and wicked rebellion that the world has seen; and, believing as we do, that the only hope of ; this country and preserving the Constitution, is by the power of the sword, we are for the most vigo- ›rosecution of the war, until all the Constitution and laws shall be enforced and obeyed in all parts of nited States; and to that end we oppose any armistice, or intervention, or mediation, or propositions ace from any quarter, so long as there shall be found a rebel in arms against the Government; and we ; all party names, lines, and issues, and recognize but two parties in this war—patriots and traitors." esolution was adopted—yeas 94, nays 65. Mr. Pendleton voting in the negative.

anuary 18, 1864.—Mr. Smith, of Kentucky, submitted a preamble and resolution, as follows:— ›as, A most desperate, wicked, and bloody Rebellion exists within the jurisdiction of the United States, ıe safety and security of personal and national liberty depend on upon its absolute and utter extinction; ore,

›solved, That it is the political, civil, moral, and sacred duty of the people to meet it, fight it, crush l forever destroy it.

r. James C. Allen moved to lay the preamble and resolution on the table, but it failed, though Mr. ›ton voting in the negative, with Wood, Voorhees, James C. Allen, Long, Harris of Maryland, Ancona, her Copperheads.

›bruary 15, 1864.—Mr. Arnold submitted the following resolution:—Resolved, That the Constitu- ıould be so amended as to abolish Slavery in the United States wherever it now exists, and to prohibit ›tence in every part thereof forever.——It was adopted by yeas, 78; nays 62; Mr. Pendleton voting in ;ative.

pril 9, 1864.—A joint resolution was offered to expel Benjamin G. Harris, a Representative from the f Maryland, for uttering the following treasonable language in that body:—"The South asked you to hem in peace. But no; you said you would bring them into subjection. That is not done yet; and God ıty grant that it never may be. I hope that you will never subjugate the South."——On the vote to the yeas were 84, nays 58—Mr. Pendleton voting in the negative.

ne 13, 1864.—Mr. Pendleton voted against the repeal of the fugitive slave act. The vote stood—yeas ys 62.

ne 15, 1864.—Mr. Pendleton voted against the joint resolution of the Senate proposing to the State s of the Constitution, so as to forever to prohibit Slavery.

"The Union must be Preserved!"
The Country above Party.

THE

NATIONAL UNION ASSOCIATION

OF OHIO.

HEADQUARTERS CATHOLIC INSTITUTE, (First Floor,)

N. W. CORRER VINE & LONGWORTH STS., CINCINNATI.

WEEKLY MEETINGS IN MOZART HAT

Each Tuesday and Saturday Night until Nov. 12, 1864.

OFFICERS.

Dr. WILLIAM SHERWOOD, *President.*
S. S. DAVIS, *Treasurer.*
JOHN D. CALDWELL, *General Secretary.*
Hon. EDWARD WOODRUFF, *Chairman Ex. Com.*

SUB-COMMITTEES.

FINANCE.

Henry Kessler, *Chairman.*
L. S. Rosenstiel,
S. C. Newton,
D. T. Woodrow,
James Dalton,
Dr. O. W. Nixon,
Eli Johnson,
S. S. Davis.

CAMPAIGN.

S. C. Newton *Chairman.*
F. J. Mayer,
C. F. Wilstach,
Geo. H. Wolff,
Charles Reakirt,
Peter Gibson,
Joseph Kirkup,
John W. Carter,
Charles Bro
Hugh McBi
E. C. Middl

HALL, SPEAKERS, &c.

Edgar Conkling, *Chairman.*
Geo H. Wolff,
Maj. R. M. Corwine,
O. H. Geffroy,
Adolph Woods,
Jacob Wolf
M. Sweeny.

DOCUMENTS, PRINTING, &c.

Hon. Ed. Woodruff,
George Graham,
A. T. Butler,
D. M. Marsh,
M. B. Haga
J. D. Caldv

EXPENDITURES AND ACCOUNTS.

Col. A. Watson, *Chairman.*
J. W. Wynne,
N. Patters

☞ Send orders for Union Documents.

JOHN D. CALDWELL, Gen.

Printed and Published by CALEB CLARK, S. W. Cor. Third & Walnut St., Cinc

www.ingramcontent.com/pod-product-compliance
Lightning Source LLC
LaVergne TN
LVHW011143110826
845150LV00008B/2483

9781418191962